The Reluctant Dragon

AN ENTERTAINMENT

for

narrator, soloists,
SATB chorus, & instrumental ensemble
(or piano)

Words by
DAVID GRANT

Music by
JOHN RUTTER

Oxford University Press

Music Department, Great Clarendon Street, Oxford OX2 6DP

PREFACE

The Reluctant Dragon, in its original form, is a children's story by Kenneth Grahame, first published in 1898 in a collection of his stories called *Dream Days.* On one level it is a charming tale about a dragon who prefers writing poetry to fighting; on another level it is an allegory about prejudice and reconciliation — a children's story for grown-ups, rather like the same author's *Wind in the Willows.*

This musical adaptation was originally written as an 'entertainment' for The King's Singers (six male voices) and the City of London Sinfonia to perform at a Christmas concert. The present published version, for four soloists, narrator and chorus, can either be performed as a concert piece or staged in various ways. Children can participate in the chorus, though some altos, tenors and basses are essential. The parts of St. George and the Dragon are intended for adult singers; the Boy is probably best sung by a boy soprano, though a female soprano or mezzo-soprano is certainly possible. The orchestral accompaniment is within the capacity of good teenage or amateur players; piano accompaniment would be adequate, with double-bass and drums if possible.

Note: Kenneth Grahame gave the story a Christmas setting. This is not, however, essential to the narrative and has been made optional here by means of alternative versions of one or two passages of the text, so that the piece may be performed at any time of year.

This piece was commissioned by Abbotsholme Arts Society with funds provided by East Midlands Arts.

INSTRUMENTATION

Keyboard 1 (Electric piano, or piano)
Keyboard 2 (Harpsichord, or piano)
Percussion 1 (Glockenspiel, vibraphone, fireman's bell)
Percussion 2 (Drum kit)
Strings (Minimum 4,3,2,2,1)

Full scores and instrumental parts are on hire.

Duration: 23 minutes

CAST

BOY   Soprano or mezzo-soprano

DRAGON   Tenor

ST. GEORGE   Baritone

VILLAGER   Baritone or bass

MASTER OF CEREMONIES   Speaking part
(can double VILLAGER)

NARRATOR   Speaking part

CHORUS   S.A.T.B.

No. 1: PROLOGUE

(Narrator and Chorus)

Words by DAVID GRANT
Music by JOHN RUTTER

*NARRATOR: This is the story of a boy, a saint, and a dragon. It happened one Christmas-time† long ago, when the world was different, and there were more dragons about than there are nowadays;

With movement, but gently (♩ = 132)

although nothing much has really changed. People are still people, good and bad; boys are still boys; and you can still find the occasional dragon. Listen, and you'll see what I mean.

A ALL VOICES
p rather gently

Once up-on a time,_____ a time long a-go;

Dream days and dra-gon days_____ when life was full of ma - gic,_____

*Narration is to start as soon as the first chord is played. It is timed to end shortly before the chorus entry.
†Alternative: "one winter's time".

B TENORS and BASSES

Read-ing myths and le-gends of the won-ders of the world.   Knights in shin-ing ar-mour bear-ing

(+Drums)

SOPRANOS and ALTOS

ban-ners all un-furled;   Tales of elves and gob-lins and the spi-rits of the woods;

Hpschd.

Mon-sters in the sea   and mon-sters on the land,   and dra - gons!_____

Str. trem.

cresc.

How he longed to meet a real, fierce, fi-ery dra-gon!

sca - ly, tai - ly, green - bod - ied, red - eyed
fire-breath-ing, fear-some, fa - bu-lous, fai-ry-tale,

dra - gon.

(Narration to overlap with last chord)

No. 2: NARRATION

(overlapping with the last chord of No. 1)

NARRATOR: ... And sooner than expected his chance came. One night the shepherd came home all of a tremble.

'It's all up with me!' he exclaimed. 'Never more can I go up on them there downs! You know that cave up there?– well, I saw this *creature* sticking half way out of the cave – as big as four cart horses and all covered with shiny scales!'

The boy yawned. 'It's all right, father...don't you worry...it's only a dragon. He won't give us any trouble. I'll go up there and have a talk with him.'

So, after tea, he did.

(ATTACCA NO.3)

No. 3: CHORUS

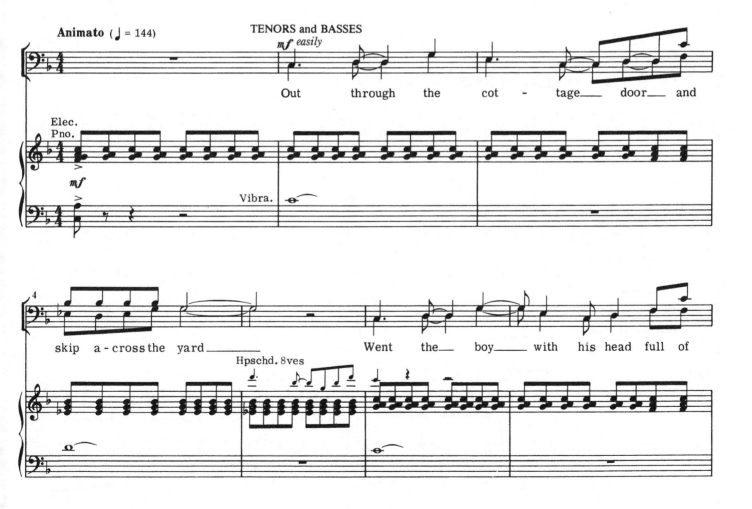

SOPRANOS and ALTOS

dra-gons breath-ing hard._____ Up a - long____ the vil - lage street and

down be - yond the inn;_____ At last his chance had come___ for real ad -

-ven - ture to be - gin._____ Up a - cross____ the hill - side all

-ven - ture, what ex - cite - ment, feels like ma - gic in the air!

Now at

34 **B** **Allegro non troppo** ($\textit{J}$ = *c.* 60)

T. and B.

last he'll know the an-swers to a ple-tho-ra of puz-zles: Does the dra-gon say his grace and such be-

SOPRANOS and ALTOS

ALL VOICES

- fore he chews and guz-zles? Does he use a ta-ble nap-kin or a knife and fork and spoon? Does he

accelerando _ _ _ _ _ _

wash his claws and whis-kers care-f'ly when he dines at noon?

SOPRANOS and ALTOS

Più mosso **C**

When he tries to eat an ice-cream does his fi-ery breath-ing melt All the

Str. pizz. +Glock.

ice and cream and send it trick-ling down his sca-ly pelt? If he sniffs at plants and flo-wers does he

TENORS and BASSES

rit. a tempo
ALL VOICES

make the blos-soms droop? Does he singe his hair and whis-kers when he blows up-on his soup? By the

D

time the boy had reached the high-est point a-mong the hills He was dream-ing all of dra-gons and their

in-stant dam-sel grills: Do they kill be - fore they grill or do they like to hear the screams Of their

Meno mosso

gent - ly roast-ing vic-tims spit-ted right a - long their seams? And in case you all are think-ing that this

rall. **Lento (in 4)**

sub-ject's done to death—Well, don't wor-ry, we shall stop now 'cos we've all run out of breath.

Segue No. 4

No. 4:

(Boy, Dragon, St. George, Chorus)

NARRATOR: And sure enough, just outside a small but comfortable cave in the hillside, a dragon lay stretched out, purring contentedly. The boy approached....

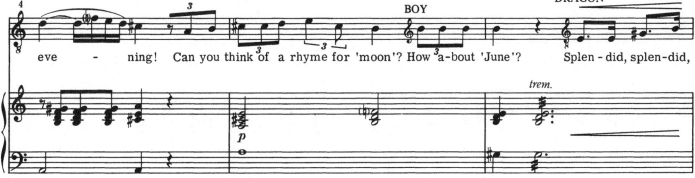

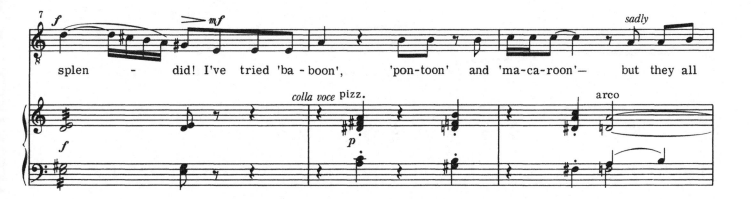

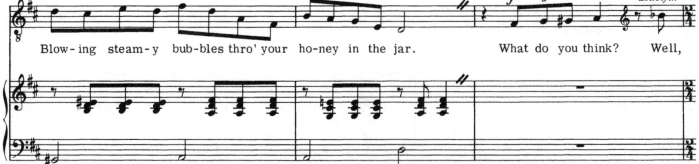

yes... Mind you, I al-so cul-ti-vate a more con-tem-p'ry style: Here's a pas-sage from my *Three Quin-*

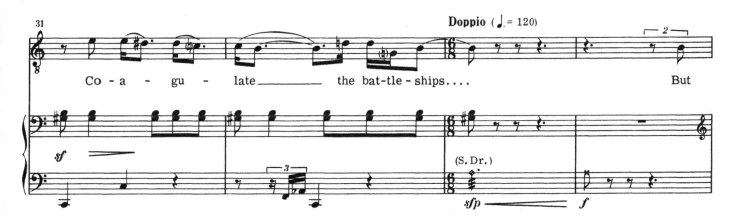

-tets: Seeth - ing___ pitch___ and bet - ting slips___

Co - a - gu - late___ the bat-tle-ships.... But

hark! What do I hear in the di - stance?___

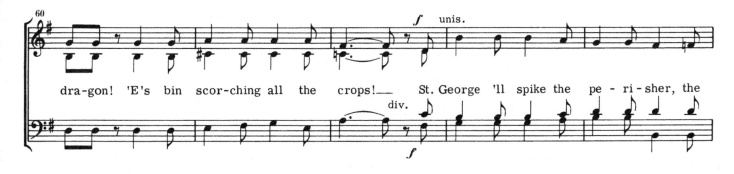

dra-gon! 'E's bin scor-ching all the crops!___ St. George 'll spike the pe - ri-sher, the

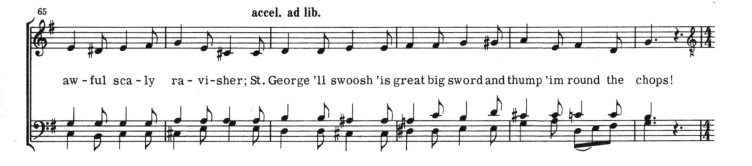

aw - ful sca - ly ra - vi-sher; St. George 'll swoosh 'is great big sword and thump 'im round the chops!

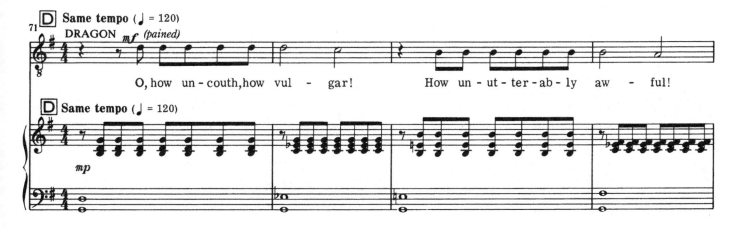

D **Same tempo** (♩ = 120)

DRAGON *mf (pained)*

O, how un-couth, how vul - gar! How un-ut-ter-ab-ly aw - ful!

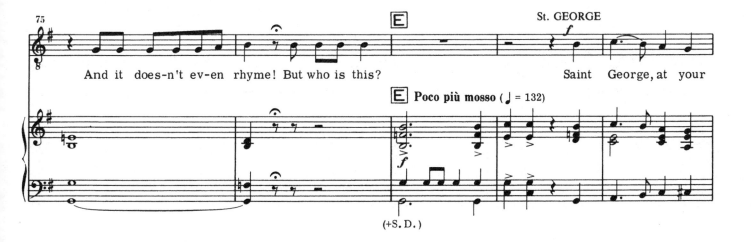

And it does-n't ev-en rhyme! But who is this?

St. GEORGE

Saint George, at your

E **Poco più mosso** (♩ = 132)

(+S. D.)

Poco meno mosso (♩ = 120)

ser - vice! The hour of reck-'ning has come, sir! Nev-er more shall you wreak your

ter - ror up - on these poor sim - ple folk! What wea-pons do you choose?

DRAGON *mp (quite faint at the thought)*

Wea - pons, dear fel-low? None, dear boy! Can't fight, won't fight! A - ny-way—

St. GEORGE

Attacca No. 5

why must I be de - feat - ed? Be - cause it's in the sto - ry!

No. 5: TRIO

(St. George, Dragon, Boy)

I'm a lit-e-ra-ry dra - gon; Not a drop, not a drop of fight in me.

A

All my Sturm and Drang is pan - to-mime; I would-n't hurt a

fly. If you're going to cut up__ rough then I'll

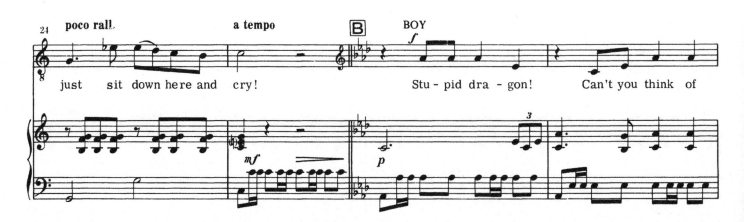

poco rall.   a tempo   **B**   BOY

just sit down here and cry! Stu - pid dra - gon! Can't you think of

what a no - ble__ sight there'd be: Nos-trils flar - ing, scales a - flash-ing, ar - mour__

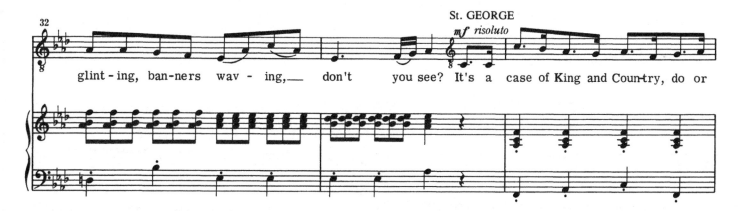

St. GEORGE

mf risoluto

glint - ing, ban-ners wav - ing,__ don't you see? It's a case of King and Coun-try, do or

die, show the flag, With a gin and t. to brace you it - 'll soon be in the bag! Ev - 'ry

cresc.

chap with a - ny feel-ing feels a qui-v'ring of his lips, When the fight-ing is all ov - er and the

cresc.

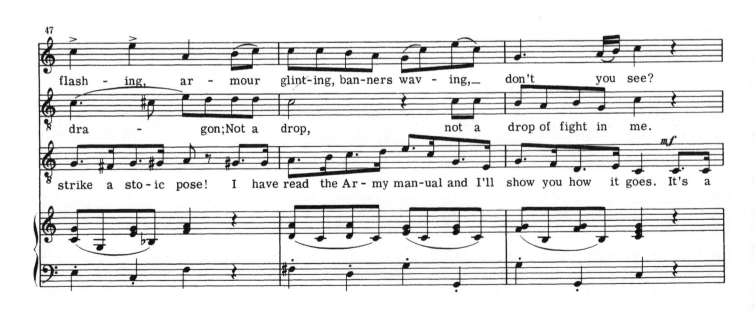

O, the splen-dour, with all the shout - ing, cheer - ing
All my Sturm and Drang is pan - to - mime; I would-n't hurt a
case of King and Coun - try, do or die, show the flag, With a gin and t. to brace you it - 'll

throng! What a no - ble sight,
fly. If you're going to cut up rough then I'll
soon be in the bag! Ev - 'ry chap with a - ny feel - ing feels a qui-v'ring of his lips When the

rall.

mp dim.

what a no - ble sight, what a no - ble
just sit down here and cry, yes I'll cry.
fight - ing is all ov - er and the foe has had his chips, when the foe has had his

mp

mp dim.

dim.

rall.

No. 6: TRIO and CHORUS

(Boy, Dragon, St. George, Chorus)

1. Dragon
2. Boy

BOY

let me have a burst,__ Oh! I'll give him quite a burst; how py - ro - tech - nic!__ 2. Then you
look as though it sticks__ so the

ah   ooh   ah_____ -ro-tech-nic!__

crowd-'ll get their kicks. I hope you're cer - tain!__

ooh   ah   And now, young fel - low,__

* or other scat syllables.

52

BOY   St.GEORGE

meant it—what a dream, O the e-mo-tion!__ Then you screw it up to pitch__ Till the

wop   bee doo bee   O the e-mo-tion!__   wop   bee doo bee

doo   bee doo bee doo bee doo O the e-mo-tion!   Doo   bee doo bee doo bee

55

DRAGON   BOY

crowd be-gins to itch__ For a kill-ing, for a vic-to-ry, for cur-tains!__   Yes, but

wop   bee doo bee doo_____   for cur-tains!__

doo   bee doo bee doo bee   doo

bit of you with no sen-sa-tion in it?— You could pin me in the wing:—See, it's

DRAGON

- tion in it— ah

real-ly on-ly skin,—That's the place, St. G., so take it to the lim-it!—

BOY

ooh ah the lim-it,—

No. 7: TOURNAMENT

(Narrator, Master of Ceremonies, Boy, Dragon, St. George, Villager, Chorus)

NARRATOR: .... And not a moment too soon. Already it was time the tournament to begin, and a crowd of villagers had gathered.

'ead___ off! We want the dra-gon! Scrag 'im, spike 'im, cut 'is froat!

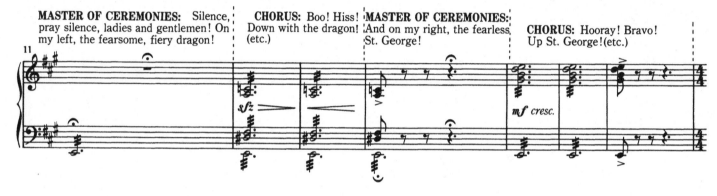

MASTER OF CEREMONIES: Silence, pray silence, ladies and gentlemen! On my left, the fearsome, fiery dragon!

CHORUS: Boo! Hiss! Down with the dragon! (etc.)

MASTER OF CEREMONIES: And on my right, the fearless St. George!

CHORUS: Hooray! Bravo! Up St. George!(etc.)

MASTER OF CEREMONIES: Right now, gentlemen, three rounds of good clean fiery combat, and may the best man win. On the word of command . . . . charge!

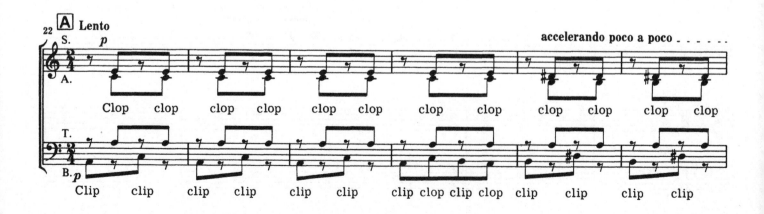

Clop clop clop clop clop clop clop clop clop clop clop clop

Clip clip clip clip clip clip clip clop clip clop clip clip clip clip

* like swords swishing through the air.

MASTER OF CEREMONIES: *(before music restarts)* Round 1: no hits; a draw!....

.... Round 2: take your marks ... charge!

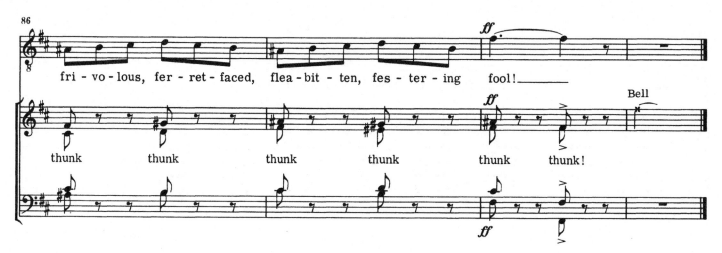

frivolous, ferret-faced, flea-bitten, festering fool!

thunk thunk thunk thunk thunk thunk!

MASTER OF CEREMONIES: Round 2: Dragon wins on points!......

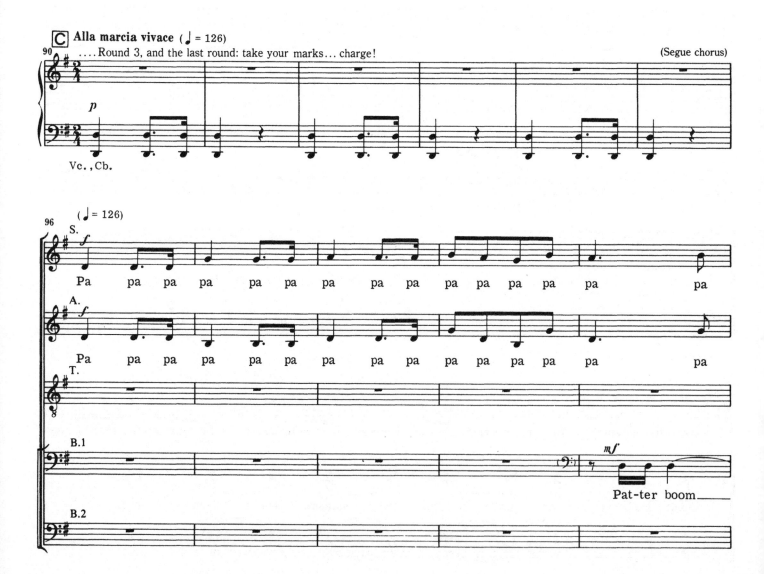

C **Alla marcia vivace** (♩ = 126)

....Round 3, and the last round: take your marks... charge!

(Segue chorus)

Vc., Cb.

(♩ = 126)

S. Pa pa pa pa pa pa pa pa pa pa pa pa pa pa pa

A. Pa pa pa pa pa pa pa pa pa pa pa pa pa pa pa

T.

B.1 Pat-ter boom

B.2

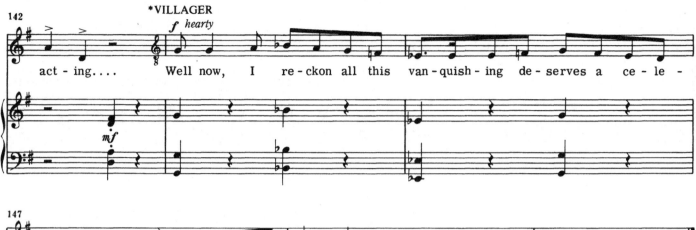

*VILLAGER

Well now, I re-ckon all this van-quish-ing de-serves a ce-le-

- bra - tion: let's have a ban - quet!

Hear, hear! Yes, yes, let's have a ban - quet!

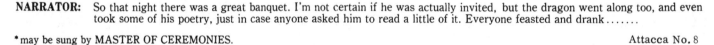

NARRATOR: So that night there was a great banquet. I'm not certain if he was actually invited, but the dragon went along too, and even took some of his poetry, just in case anyone asked him to read a little of it. Everyone feasted and drank.......

*may be sung by MASTER OF CEREMONIES.

Attacca No. 8

No. 8: BANQUET FUGUE
(Chorus)

Lively, in 2 (♩ = c. 96)

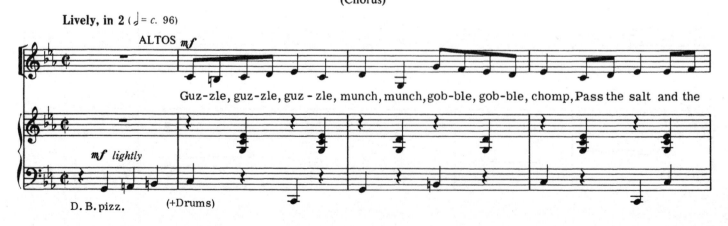

ALTOS

Guz-zle, guz-zle, guz-zle, munch, munch, gob-ble, gob-ble, chomp, Pass the salt and the

D. B. pizz. (+Drums)

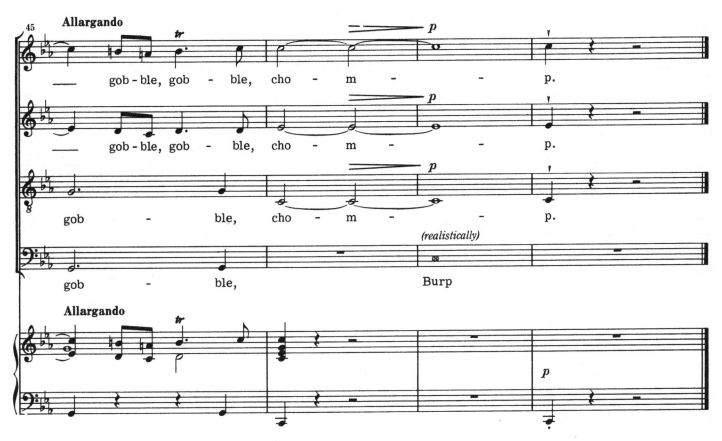

No. 9: FINALE

(Narrator, St. George, Chorus)

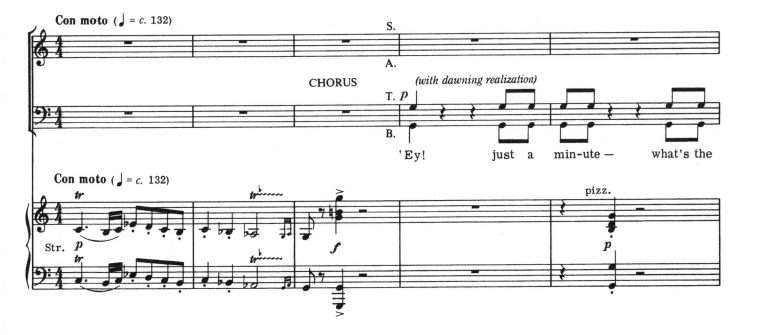

I thought St. George had slain him once and for dra-gon do-'in' 'ere?

all..... cut off his 'ead! Cut off his head? I can't do that!

He's a jol-ly good chap. I'll give him a stern talk-ing-to: now

2. So can we get it right_____ this time?

Let's find a way to start a-gain.____

Pos - si- bly.   An-oth-er chance in sight?_____   Take things ea - si-ly.

Is there time to   care   a - gain,   Time to hope and share a-gain?____

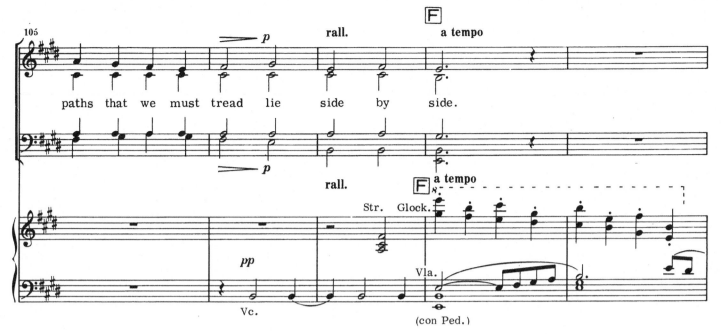

paths that we must tread lie side by side.

*NARRATOR: So at length the banquet ended. They set off up the hill arm in arm, the saint, the boy, and the dragon. The lights in the little village

began to go out; but there were stars, and a late moon, as they climbed the downs together. Soon they reached the top, and it was time for their ways to part.

They stood silent for a moment; then wished each other goodnight; and — a Merry Christmas. †

* Narration is to start during this bar. It is timed to end in the penultimate bar.
†Alternative text: "wished each other goodnight; and — sweet dreams".

Printed by Halstan